The Velveteen Rabbit
Coloring Book

A storybook to be colored in

With captions lifted from the original text by Margery Williams

Illustrated by Tien

Little Simon
Published by Simon & Schuster, Inc., New York

Illustrations copyright © 1984 by Tien Ho. All rights reserved including the right of reproduction in whole or in part in any form. Published by LITTLE SIMON, a Division of Simon & Schuster, Inc., Simon & Schuster Building, 1230 Avenue of the Americas, New York, N.Y. 10020. Manufactured in the United States of America. LITTLE SIMON and colophon are trademarks of Simon & Schuster, Inc. ISBN 0-671-49669-7

10

THERE WAS ONCE A VELVETEEN RABBIT, AND IN THE beginning he was really splendid. He was fat and bunchy, as a rabbit should be; his coat was spotted brown and white, he had real thread whiskers, and his ears were lined with pink sateen.

For a long time he lived in the toy cupboard or on the nursery floor, and no one thought very much about him.... The mechanical toys were very superior, and looked down upon everyone else.

The only person who was kind to him at all was the Skin Horse.

[He would wisely counsel the Rabbit, saying], "When a child loves you for a long, long time, not just to play with, but REALLY loves you, then you become Real."

The Rabbit sighed. He thought it would be a long time before this magic called Real happened to him.

There was a person called Nana who ruled the nursery. Sometimes she took no notice of the playthings lying about, and sometimes, for no reason whatever, she went swooping about like a great wind and hustled them away in cupboards. She called this "tidying up," and the playthings all hated it, especially the tin ones.

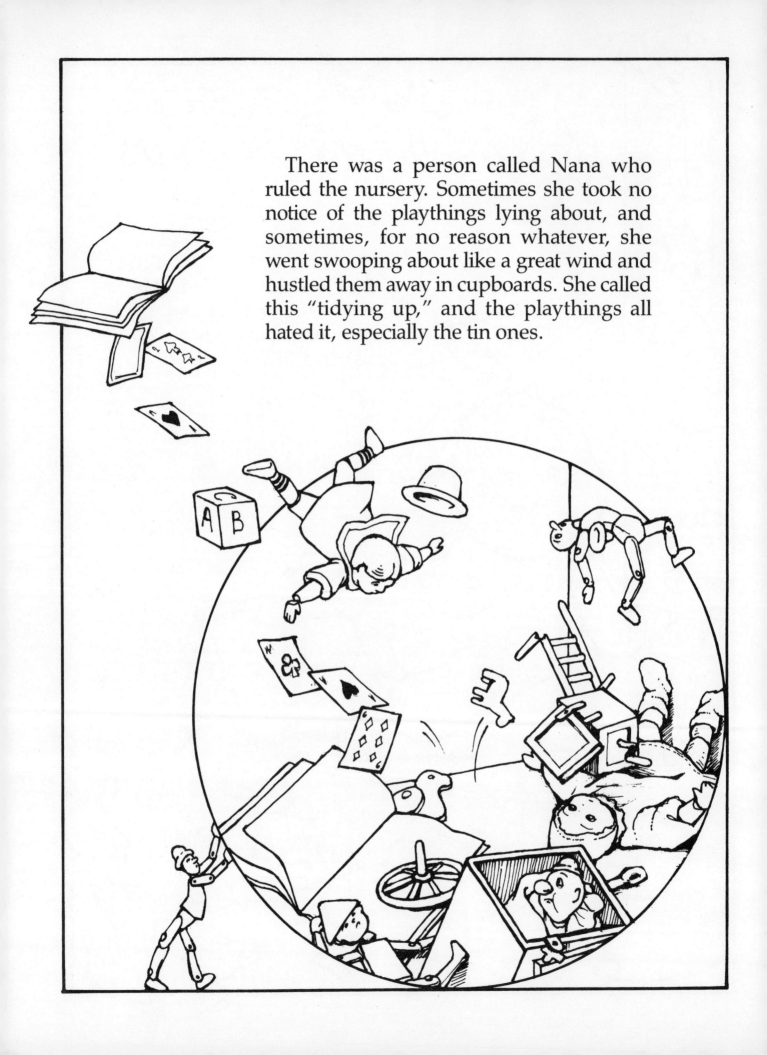

The Rabbit didn't mind it so much, for wherever he was thrown ...

he came down soft.

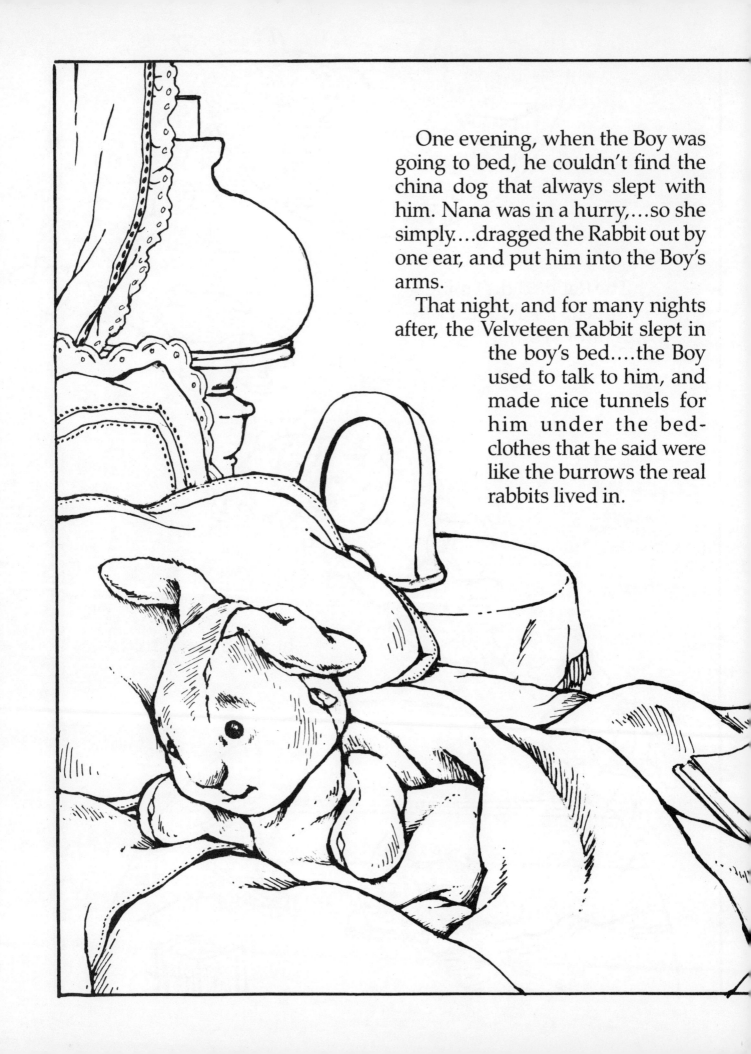

One evening, when the Boy was going to bed, he couldn't find the china dog that always slept with him. Nana was in a hurry,....so she simply....dragged the Rabbit out by one ear, and put him into the Boy's arms.

That night, and for many nights after, the Velveteen Rabbit slept in the boy's bed....the Boy used to talk to him, and made nice tunnels for him under the bed-clothes that he said were like the burrows the real rabbits lived in.

Spring came, and [the Boy and the Rabbit] had long days in the garden, for wherever the Boy went the Rabbit went too.

[The little Rabbit] had rides in the wheelbarrow, and picnics on the grass, and lovely fairy huts built for him under the raspberry canes behind the flower border.

Once, when the boy was called away suddenly to go out to tea, the Rabbit was left out on the lawn until long after dusk, and Nana had to come and look for him with the candle because the Boy couldn't go to sleep unless he was there. He was wet through with the dew and quite earthy....

The Boy sat up in bed and stretched out his hands.
"Give me my Bunny!" he said...."He isn't a toy. He's REAL!"
When the little Rabbit heard that, he was happy, for he knew that what the Skin Horse had said was true at last.

He was Real.

That was a wonderful summer!

[The Boy] took the Velveteen Rabbit with him [into the wood], and before he wandered off to pick flowers,...he always made the Rabbit a little nest somewhere...where he would be quite cosy....

One evening, while the Rabbit was lying there alone,...
he saw two strange beings creep out of the tall bracken
near him.

They were rabbits like himself, but quite furry and brand-new....

"Why don't you get up and play with us?" one of them asked.

"I don't feel like it," said the Rabbit, for he didn't want to explain that he had no clockwork.

"Ho!" said the furry rabbit. "It's as easy as anything."

And he gave a big hop sideways and stood on his hind legs....

And [then] he began to whirl around and dance, till the little Rabbit got quite dizzy.

"He doesn't smell right!" [one of the rabbits] exclaimed. "He isn't a rabbit at all! He isn't real!"

"I *am* Real!" said the little Rabbit. "I am Real! The Boy said so!" And he nearly began to cry.

Just then there was a sound of footsteps, and the Boy ran past near them, and with a stamp of feet and a flash of white tails the two strange rabbits disappeared.

"Come back and play with me!" called the little Rabbit. "Oh, do come back! I *know* I am Real!"....

For a long time he lay very still, watching the bracken, and hoping that they would come back. But they never returned....

Weeks passed, and the little Rabbit grew very old and shabby, but the Boy loved him just as much.

And then, one day, the Boy was ill....

It was a long weary time, for the Boy was too ill to play,... but [the Velveteen Rabbit] snuggled down patiently, and looked forward to the time when the Boy should be well again, and they would go out in the garden amongst the flowers and the butterflies and play splendid games in the raspberry thicket like they used to.

And presently the fever turned, and the Boy got better. He was able to sit up in bed and look at picture books, while the little Rabbit cuddled close at his side.

The Boy was going to the seaside tomorrow. Everything was arranged, and now it only remained to carry out the doctor's orders....the little Rabbit lay under the bedclothes, with just his head peeping out, and listened. The room was to be disinfected, and all the books and toys that the Boy had played with in bed must be burnt.

"Hurrah!" thought the little Rabbit. "Tomorrow we shall go to the seaside!" for the Boy had often talked of the seaside, and he wanted very much to see the big waves coming in, and the tiny crabs, and the sand castles.

Just then Nana caught sight of him.

"How about his old Bunny?" she asked.

"*That?*" said the doctor. "Why, it's a mass of scarlet fever germs!—Burn it at once...."

And so the little Rabbit was put into a sack with the old picture-books and a lot of rubbish....

That night the Boy slept in a dif-
ferent bedroom, and he had a new
bunny to sleep with him. It was a
splendid bunny, all white plush with
real glass eyes....

And while the Boy was asleep, dreaming of the seaside, the little Rabbit lay among the old picture-books,....and he felt very lonely....And a tear, a real tear, trickled down his little shabby velvet nose and fell to the ground.

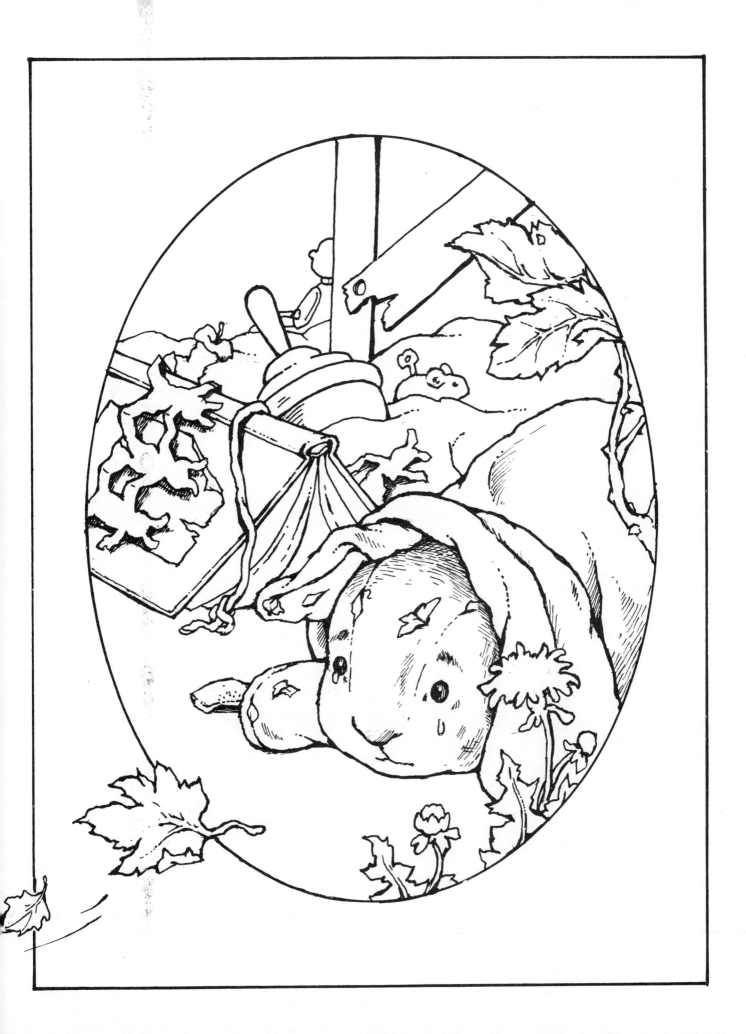

And then a strange thing happened. For where the tear had fallen a flower grew out of the ground, a mysterious flower, not at all like any that grew in the garden....And presently the blossom opened, and out of it there stepped a fairy.

"I am the nursery magic Fairy," she said. "I take care of all the playthings that the children have loved. When they are old and worn out and the children don't need them any more, then I come and take them away with me and turn them into Real."

And she held the little Rabbit close in her arms and flew with him into the woods.

In the open glade between the tree-trunks the wild rabbits danced with their shadows on the velvet grass, but when they saw the Fairy they all stopped dancing and stood round in a ring to stare at her.

"I've brought you a new playfellow," the Fairy said. "You must be very kind to him and teach him all he needs to know in Rabbitland, for he is going to live with you for ever and ever!"

And he found that he actually had hind legs!....[The little Rabbit] gave one leap and the joy of using those hind legs was so great that he went springing about the turf on them....

He was a real rabbit at last, at home with the other rabbits.

Autumn passed and winter, and in the spring, when the days grew warm and sunny, the Boy went out to play in the wood behind the house. And while he was playing, two rabbits crept out from the bracken and peeped at him.

"Why, [that one] looks just like my old Bunny that was lost when I had scarlet fever!" [the Boy whispered aloud].

But he never knew that it really was his own Bunny, come back to look at the child who had first helped him to be Real.